Discovering
The North Pennines
Keith Durham

Photographs by
Keith Durham & Christopher Hartnell

Photographic Acknowledgements:
Front Cover: Evening light above Rookhope. *Photo:* Keith Durham.
Lead Miners archive photo: page 7 courtesy Nenthead Mines Heritage Trust.
John Wesley photo: page 21 courtesy Weardale Museum, Ireshopeburn.
North Pennines map. Page ii courtesy North Pennines AONB Partnership.
Design: Ian Scott Design.
Printed in Great Britain by Printers (Coast) Ltd., Newcastle upon Tyne.
Text and photographs © Northern Heritage 2004.

ISBN No.0-9544777-2-3
Northern Heritage
Units 7&8 New Kennels, Blagdon Estate, Seaton Burn,
Newcastle upon Tyne,
NE13 6DB
www.northern-heritage.co.uk

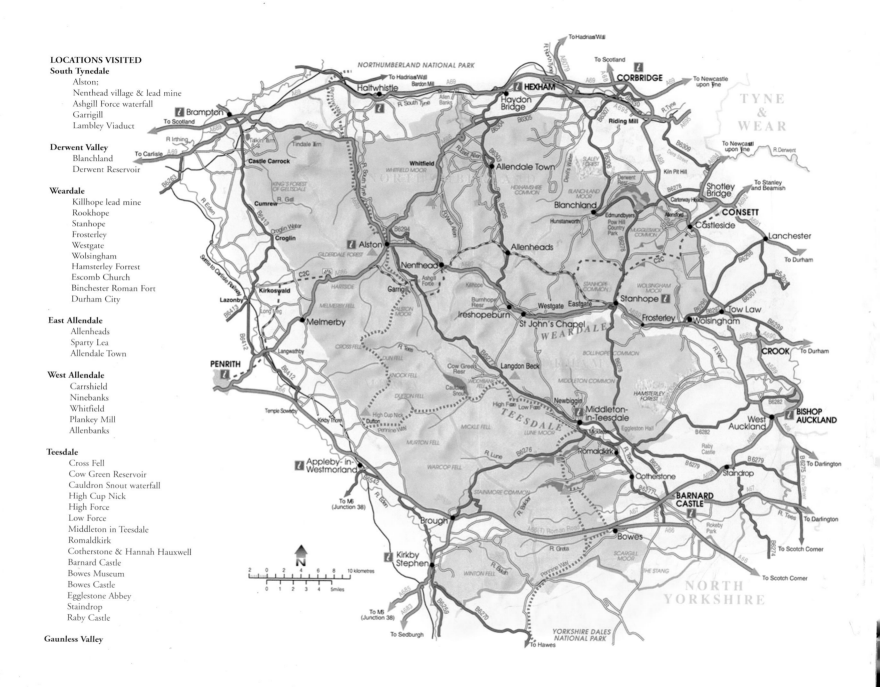

LOCATIONS VISITED

South Tynedale
- Alston;
- Nenthead village & lead mine
- Ashgill Force waterfall
- Garrigill
- Lambley Viaduct

Derwent Valley
- Blanchland
- Derwent Reservoir

Weardale
- Killhope lead mine
- Rookhope
- Stanhope
- Frosterley
- Westgate
- Wolsingham
- Hamsterley Forrest
- Escomb Church
- Binchester Roman Fort
- Durham City

East Allendale
- Allenheads
- Sparty Lea
- Allendale Town

West Allendale
- Carrshield
- Ninebanks
- Whitfield
- Plankey Mill
- Allenbanks

Teesdale
- Cross Fell
- Cow Green Reservoir
- Cauldron Snout waterfall
- High Cup Nick
- High Force
- Low Force
- Middleton in Teesdale
- Romaldkirk
- Cotherstone & Hannah Hauxwell
- Barnard Castle
- Bowes Museum
- Bowes Castle
- Egglestone Abbey
- Staindrop
- Raby Castle

Gaunless Valley

THE NORTH PENNINES

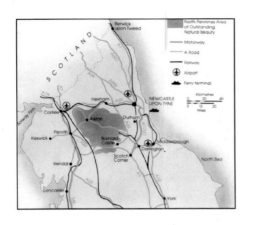

*T*he North Pennines is a truly special place. Here, in this dramatic landscape of rugged moors, gentle dales and historic towns and villages, you will find a rich industrial and social heritage, an abundance of flora and fauna and a wealth of natural beauty. There is so much to explore and discover; mighty castles, ancient churches, thundering waterfalls, scenic reservoirs, long distance trails and quiet riverside walks. Traditional, stone built villages are scattered along the valley floors and the highest roads in England afford breathtaking views as they climb over the lofty moorland ridges that separate the dales. A challenging stretch of the Pennine Way snakes across the North Pennines and an increasing number of cyclists pass through this exhilarating area on their journey from 'Coast to Coast'.

Lying at the hub of three areas of national importance, the Lake District, the Northumberland National Park and the Yorkshire Dales, it comes as no surprise to discover that the North Pennines has been designated as one of England's largest "Areas of Outstanding Natural Beauty". It has also, with good reason, been designated as a European Geopark.

Geologically, the North Pennines is formed by what is known as the Alston Block. The rocks are made up of thin layers of coal, sandstone, shale and limestone, which were laid down as sediments in tropical seas hundreds of millions of years ago. These layers give many of the dale sides their characteristic, stepped appearance.

Later, volcanic activity forced molten Quartz Dolerite into cracks in the overlying layers of sediment and during recent ice ages, the soft sediments were scoured away, revealing the harder Quartz Dolerite. Known as the Whin Sill, it can be seen in places such as Cauldron Snout, High Force, Cronkley Scar and High Cup Nick. Also forced upwards from the earth's core into cracks was mineral bearing molten rock, which cooled to form deposits of silver, rich lead ore and iron ore. It is the presence of these minerals that gave rise to the mining industry that has had such an impact on the North Pennines landscape.

For botanists and ornithologists, the North Pennines is a veritable paradise. In the spring, the sheer number and variety of breeding birds is astonishing. This is the most important upland area in England for black grouse and red grouse and on the valley floors, hay meadows provide a feeding ground for species such as linnet, grey partridge and lapwing. Other breeds frequenting the area include the hen harrier, merlin, short-eared owl, oystercatcher, redshank and curlew.

In the upland areas of the North Pennines, on the limestone grasslands, the region's geology has nurtured many rare plant species such as Teesdale violet, blue gentian, birds-eye primrose and globe flower.

People first came to the Dales around 7,000 years ago when nomadic hunters had temporary campsites in the area and the dense woodland that covered the land was gradually cleared for firewood, building and grazing. From prehistoric times until the enclosure of common land in the 1700's, cattle were moved between upland and lowland grazing on a seasonal basis and over thousands of years, this constant movement of livestock created 'drove ways' that later became the winding country lanes that so characterise the landscape of the North Pennine Dales today.

When the Romans arrived around 80AD, they built military roads and forts across the region and also began to mine the area's rich deposits of lead ore. After the Romans left in the fifth century, a succession of invaders settled in the Dales including the Angles, the Danes and finally the Normans, who arrived in about 1070. They brought with them a feudal system of land control and began to build the magnificent churches, castles, and cathedrals that still dominate our skylines today.

Although each dale retains its own quite unique character, there are unifying elements that bind the North Pennines into a geographical area, particularly in the way that it's industrial past has shaped the landscape.

Ever since man first settled the Pennine dales, the area's rich mineral deposits had always been excavated in small amounts, but in the 19th century, as the Industrial Revolution took hold, these minerals, which were essential in the processing of iron and steel, began to be extracted from the earth in ever increasing volumes. At first, packhorses were used for transportation, but with the advent of George Stephenson's steam driven Locomotive, railways were constructed throughout the dales, and minerals were rapidly transported to the voracious iron and steel furnaces in the Tyne and Tees valleys.

Once the full potential of the railway became apparent, mining operations rapidly expanded, and by Victorian times, the North Pennine area was the world's largest lead ore field. Nowadays, the North Pennines has a population of about 12,000 people, which is less than half it's population in 1861. At that time, 27,000 people lived and worked here and today's tranquil landscape was a hive of activity as men hacked out of the earth vast quantities of iron ore, limestone and lead.

It is hard to believe that this beautiful area was once at the cutting edge of the industrial revolution, for much of this landscape has now been restored. Most of the unsightly scarring has all but disappeared and packhorse routes and railway lines have been transformed into excellent walks and heritage trails, where visitors can explore the fascinating remnants of this dramatic period.

THE SOUTH TYNE, ALSTON AND NENTHEAD

An imaginative, monolithic monument sculptured by Gilbert Ward and erected in 2002 marks the site where the river South Tyne rises at Tyne Head. Here, the river begins its life as little more than a trickle, but a short distance downstream, it is joined by the Ashgill, a lovely tributary which plunges majestically over Ashgill Force before flowing into the South Tyne. Ashgill Force was once the site of a lead ore washing plant and the Ashgill Horse Level was one of the richest lead ore veins in the area. Nowadays, the waterfall is a much visited local beauty spot.

The South Tyne continues its meandering journey, passing the village of Garrigill before reaching

Far left: **Gilbert Ward's sculpture at Tyne Head, source of the South Tyne.**

Left: **Garrigill.**

1

Alston, a place from which many visitors begin their journey to the North Pennines. The town is perched high on a landscape of sweeping moorland and the air here is fresh, clean - and generally quite bracing. It's not really surprising, for as a milestone at Town Foot reminds us, we are standing 921 feet above sea level and Alston justly lays claim to being Englands highest market town.

Alston takes its name from the Pennine grey stone - or "auldstone" - which can be seen in its rugged cobbled streets. The fine Market Cross and mellow, stone roofed market place give the town a pleasant and distinctly 19th century air. Church Gaytes House was built in 1681 and picturesque dwellings at the Butts, now tastefully renovated, date back to the 17th century.

The surrounding landscape is one of the richest mineral depositories in Britain, and lead, silver, zinc, iron, and copper ores have all been found and mined here. In the 19th century, the mining industry was serviced by a branch railway that ran from Alston to Haltwhistle, where it joined the Newcastle to Carlisle line. This arrangement lasted for 124 years before the line finally closed in 1976.

The station is now home to the Alston - South Tynedale Railway, a private enterprise run by dedicated railway enthusiasts. In 1983, having restored a number of steam and diesel

Far left: **Looking through Ashgill Force, from the path that goes behind the waterfall.**
Left: **Ashgill Force.**

2

Above: **Seven Sisters Waterfall.**

Above: **Alston Station.**

Right: **Market Place.**

locomotives, they succeeded in opening a narrow gauge line along part of the old track bed. Now, on most days between Easter and October, visitors can take the two and a quarter mile train ride from Alston to Kirkhaugh and along the way, enjoy some fine scenic views across the South Tyne Valley.

Although the prosperity that Alston enjoyed in the heyday of the leadmining boom vanished long ago, that wealth is now being regenerated by a thriving tourist industry. The Town Hall houses the busy Tourist Information Centre and each summer, an increasing number of visitors can be found browsing through Alston's shops and craft galleries, or exploring the towns quaint cobbled streets, narrow passageways and twisting lanes.

A short walk from the town brings you to the lovely Seven Sisters Waterfall. Here, peace and tranquillity reign, and in the spring, the surrounding hillsides are decked with purple

Far left: **The Butts, Alston.**
Left: **Church Gaytes House.**

Above: **Alston in early Autumn.**

orchids, wild pansies and marsh marigolds.

Below Alston, an important landmark on the west bank of the South Tyne is the hill fort of Whitley Castle. Built by the Romans in order to control local tribes, it was used as a base from which to extend their influence in the North Pennines and to protect their sources of lead ore.

Above: **Lambley Viaduct.**

Spanning the South Tyne between Lambley and Coanwood stands the magnificent Lambley Viaduct. Built by the engineer Sir George Barclay Bruce to carry the Alston to Haltwhistle branch line across the South Tyne, this awesome structure towers 110 feet above the river. It was opened in 1852 by the Newcastle and Carlisle Railway Company and has recently been restored to its former glory by the North Pennines Heritage Trust.

Further downriver stands Featherstone Castle, which was built in 1290 by Thomas de Featherstone. The Featherstones were a powerful local family and at some point, Thomas decide to abandon his castle higher up in the hills and moved to this flat riverside area known as a 'haugh'.

Subsequently, the family name became extended to Featherstonehaugh.

From Featherstonehaugh, the South Tyne flows swiftly through Haltwhistle and Haydon Bridge and finally joins the North Tyne at Warden, near Hexham

An important tributary of the South Tyne is the River Nent, which rises near the village of Nenthead. Set amidst some of the wildest and most breathtaking scenery in the British Isles, Nenthead is without doubt the highest village in England. Most of the mining around Nenthead was carried out under the auspices of the Quaker London Leadmining

Company. The first smelt mill had been built in 1737 and initially, miners and their dependents lived in abject poverty, making homes wherever they could. A good many of them lived in old farm buildings, outhouses and even lean-to's on Alston Moor. Eventually, however, around 1820, the company made working arrangements a little more permanent, building 35 cottages, a school, a chapel, a clocktower and a market hall. The company also drained the surrounding high pastures, which allowed the miners to cultivate smallholdings and grow their own food. To this day, some of their cottages still hug the surrounding hillsides. Now derelict and roofless, they are touching memorials to the hardy men and women who scraped out an existence on these bleak and lonely moors 200 years ago.

You can get some idea of the conditions the miners worked in at the Nenthead Mines Heritage Centre where there are six exhibition buildings that tell the fascinating story of the lead and zinc mining industry. Here, visitors can operate a number of large water wheels and can venture underground and experience the world of the 17th century leadminer.

Nenthead is also home to an incredible feat of early industrial engineering - the Nent Force Level. Built in 1776, this mine drainage channel, driven into the ground between Nenthead and Alston, is almost 5 miles long and took an incredible 66 years to build. The channel was designed to drain water from the surrounding high fells, which would

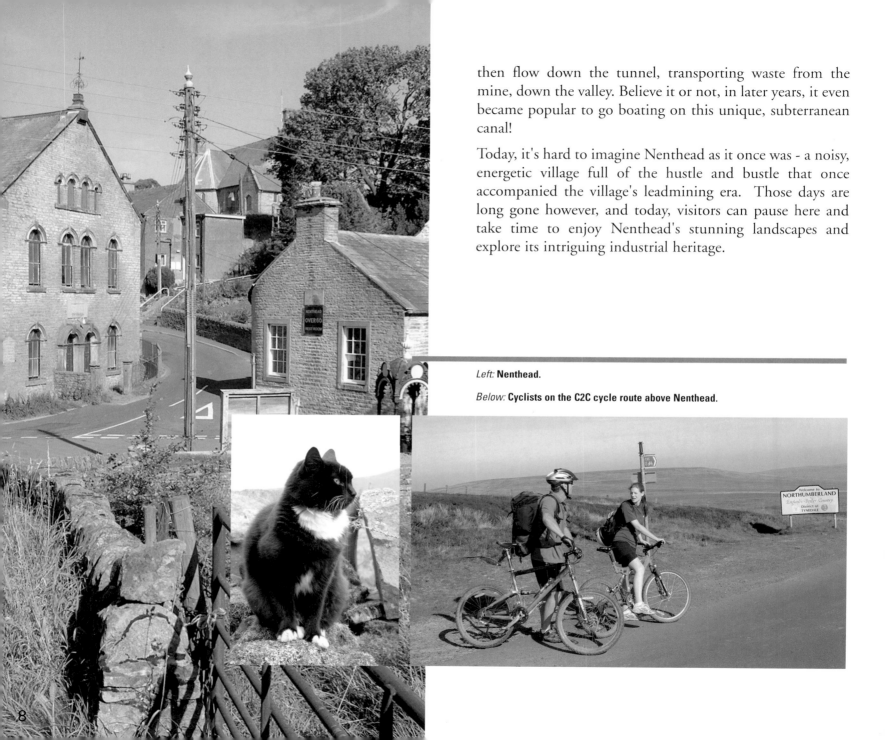

then flow down the tunnel, transporting waste from the mine, down the valley. Believe it or not, in later years, it even became popular to go boating on this unique, subterranean canal!

Today, it's hard to imagine Nenthead as it once was - a noisy, energetic village full of the hustle and bustle that once accompanied the village's leadmining era. Those days are long gone however, and today, visitors can pause here and take time to enjoy Nenthead's stunning landscapes and explore its intriguing industrial heritage.

Left: **Nenthead.**

Below: **Cyclists on the C2C cycle route above Nenthead.**

THE DERWENT VALLEY

Tucked away in the eastern corner of the North Pennines is the beautiful Derwent Valley. Here, hidden away in the far south east of Northumberland, under a cliff named Gibraltar Rock, the union of the Beldon Burn and the Nookton Burn gives birth to the river Derwent.

Downstream, where a lofty bridge leads the traveller from Northumberland into County Durham stands Blanchland, surely one of the prettiest villages in the North Pennines. Sheltered, remote and the very image of tranquillity, Blanchland was the place chosen by Walter de Bolbeck in 1165 to build an abbey for twelve white canons of the Premonstratensian Order. They named the abbey "blanche lande" after the white glade at Cherbourg from which their order originated, and no doubt, in recognition of the white

habits worn by their members. Nowadays, picturesque stone cottages cluster around what was probably the cloister of the abbey and that part of the abbot's residence where guests would have been accommodated is now home to the Lord Crewe Arms. It seems somehow appropriate that the refectory of the old abbey should have been turned into an inn where hot food and hospitality still attract visitors all year round. The building has many interesting architectural features and in the former kitchen there is a fine old fireplace with a cunningly concealed "priest hole" hidden behind it. This is a legacy from the late 16th century, when Catholicism was banned and priests were exiled from the country and forbidden to return under pain of death. In spite of such draconian measures, many did return and Catholic families such as the Forsters, who lived here in those times and still practiced their religion in secret, gave sanctuary to these priests and in times of peril, hid them

9

from the authorities.

Blanchland was much troubled by Scots raiders in the Border Wars and the massive 15th century gatehouse still stands guard at the entrance to the village square. The abbey lay in ruins for 200 years after the dissolution of the monasteries and the parish church, restored on a much smaller scale in the 18th century, is the main surviving relic. At about the same time, much of the village was rebuilt in order to house lead miners, who worked on the surrounding moors.

From Blanchland, the river Derwent flows east, before tumbling into the Derwent Reservoir. At three and a half miles long and up to a mile wide, the Derwent is Northumberland's second largest reservoir. Constructed in 1967, the reservoir is bounded by spectacular stretches of moorland, rolling conifer plantations and gentle farmland. Part of the reservoir is protected as a nature reserve and large numbers of wildfowl and waders overwinter here. The water is stocked with rainbow and brown trout and is a popular venue for fishermen. The Derwent is also home to the largest sailing club in the North East and there are superb vantage points around the reservoir where sightseers can admire a variety of sailing craft being put through their paces.

Behind the high dam, the River Derwent leaves the North Pennines and begins the final leg of its journey, before joining the River Tyne at Derwent Haugh near Blaydon.

Left: **The picturesque village of Blanchland.**

THE ALLENDALES

To the southwest, across a wild and lonely region lies the remote village of Allenheads, the highest inhabited village in the North Pennines. Here, the weather can be fickle and the Allenheads Inn is often a welcome sight for tourists and travellers. Hillwalkers, cyclists and skiers come here now, but at one time, Allenheads was a busy industrial centre and its mines churned out a seventh of all the lead produced in Britain. In fact, the village was of enough importance to merit the introduction of electricity - even ahead of the city of Newcastle! Now, some of the buildings associated with the leadmining industry have been utilised for modern ventures, such as the craft centre and the popular Hemmel café.

One building however, the Armstrong Engine House, contains a fascinating piece of history from those boomtown days. Designed by the brilliant Victorian engineer, Thomas Sopwith, it is an innovative piston driven engine produced locally to replace the slower water driven wheels used in the mines and thus speed up production. This unique hydraulic machine worked on much the same principal as a steam driven engine, but used waterpower that was channelled from a number of reservoirs above the village.

Nearby is the curiously named hamlet of Dirt Pot. Here, in the 19th century at the height of the leadmining boom, a picturesque row of stone cottages was home to the village's lead smelters and their families.

One of many abandoned cottages to be found in the Allendale area .

Above Dirt Pot, and past the Dodd Reservoir, is a pack horse trail known as the Carriers Way. Hardy little dales ponies each carried about 2cwt. of lead ore along this route, which runs all the way from Killhope to the smelting mills at Coalcleugh Bridge. Following the trail across the high fells makes a grand walk for anyone with the stamina, and the spectacular views down the length of Allendale will more than reward the effort.

Like so many other villages in

Above: **Allendale Town square.**
Left: **The Church of St. Cuthbert, Allendale.**

the Northern Pennines, Allenheads suffered a drastic decline in its fortunes when the leadmining industry collapsed, but now it is drawing a new kind of strength and prosperity from all those who love the outdoors and come here to explore this wild and breathtaking landscape.

Following the dale northwards past the hamlets of Sparty Lea and Sinderhope, the East Allen cuts its way through a stunning panorama of wild moorland summits, deeply wooded ravines and remote farmsteads, which gradually give way to a gentler, rural landscape.

Here, overlooking the river, stands the town of Allendale. Like Allenheads, this town - which is more of a village nowadays - was once a hive of activity in the leadmining era. The spacious market square, which lends the town much of its character, has a distinctly Edwardian air and is surrounded by tall, attractive stone houses and a number

Above: **Abandoned Lime kilns, above Allenheads.**
Photo: © Countryside Agency/Charlie Hedley 03-4625

Right: **West Allen valley.**

of hotels and inns. Allendale lays claim to be at the geographical centre of Britain and to reflect the idea, there is a 19th century sundial on the church of St. Cuthbert, displaying the latitude of the town.

The town is also justly famous for its "Tar Barls" ceremony, which is held on New Years Eve. In a ceremony that predates Christianity, locals dressed in colourful costumes and with blackened faces, parade through the town carrying blazing tar barrels on their heads. The parade converges in the market square and just before midnight, the barrels are ceremonially thrown onto a massive bonfire. Large numbers of spectators flock to the town on New Years Eve and the ceremony is generally preceded and followed by much dancing, merrymaking and numerous visits to the local hostelries.

In days gone by, Allendale was also famous for the "hirings"

13

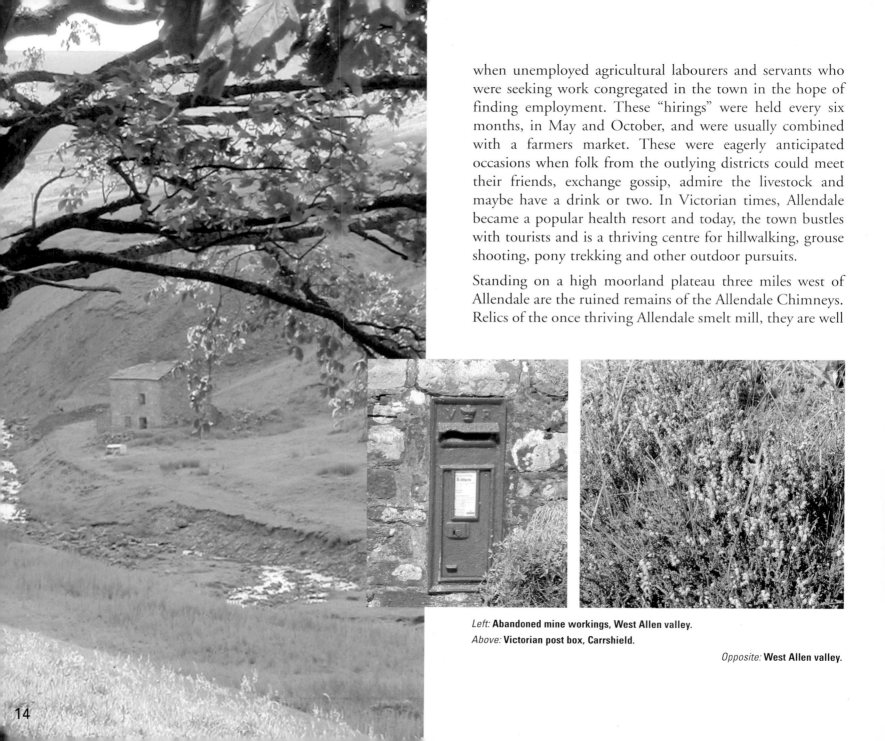

when unemployed agricultural labourers and servants who were seeking work congregated in the town in the hope of finding employment. These "hirings" were held every six months, in May and October, and were usually combined with a farmers market. These were eagerly anticipated occasions when folk from the outlying districts could meet their friends, exchange gossip, admire the livestock and maybe have a drink or two. In Victorian times, Allendale became a popular health resort and today, the town bustles with tourists and is a thriving centre for hillwalking, grouse shooting, pony trekking and other outdoor pursuits.

Standing on a high moorland plateau three miles west of Allendale are the ruined remains of the Allendale Chimneys. Relics of the once thriving Allendale smelt mill, they are well

Left: **Abandoned mine workings, West Allen valley.**
Above: **Victorian post box, Carrshield.**

Opposite: **West Allen valley.**

known landmarks and from this elevated vantage point, panoramic views of the surrounding countryside abound.

To the west, across Allendale common, amidst a high expanse of rough grazing pasture and moorland, the sparkling West Allen rises near Coalcleugh.

Coursing past Carrshield, the river twists and turns, forging its way through a bleak and remote landscape. This stretch of the West Allen valley still bears the scars of industrial dereliction and scattered across its slopes lie the melancholy ruins of long abandoned lead miners cottages.

Further downriver, as the valley begins to widen, the landscape becomes greener and increasingly pastoral. Here nestles the sheltered hamlet of Ninebanks. Rustic cottages and some fine stone houses line the quiet road which passes through the village and the picturesque remains of a medieval pele tower stand in mute testimony to more troubled times. Nowadays, however, it would be difficult to find a more peaceful haven.

Flowing ever northwards, the West Allen passes the nearby village of Whitfield, before eventually merging with the East Allen River.

Whitfield can trace its origins back to Saxon times and in the 12th century, William the Lion of Scotland granted the manor of Whitfield to the canons of Hexham. At the dissolution of the monasteries, however, it passed to the Whitfield family and in the 19th century the estate came into the hands of the Blackett-Ords.

Their commitment to the parish is reflected in the sturdy 'Blackett Bridge' on the Ninebanks road and in the gifting of the striking parish church. Built in 1860, the church was described in 1884 as "very chaste and beautiful" and is dedicated as the Church of the Divine Trinity. The lofty stone spire is 120 feet high and the interior of the church, which houses various memorials to the Blackett-Ord family, is illuminated by a number of beautifully muted, stained glass windows.

A short distance downstream from the confluence of the two rivers, the Allen passes under the lofty arch of Cupola Bridge. An early 19th century smelting mill once stood nearby and as part of the ore smelting process, the mill

employed a low-arched, reverbaratory furnace called a 'cupola', from which the bridge takes its name.

High above the Allen, across a patchwork of wooded copses and gently sloping fields, a passer-by may well chance upon scenes of rural life that would not be out of place 100 years ago. John Dodd and his family, made famous by the acclaimed TV series "The Last Horsemen", are probably the last farmers in the North Pennines to still harness horse power whilst carrying out the timeless cycle of traditional farming. The sight of these dauntless men and their hardy Clydesdale horses working the land together in perfect harmony is a precious reminder of a way of life that has almost vanished from our isles.

Above: **Former smithy, Whitfield.**
Above right: **Steeple of 'Church of the Divine Trinity', Whitfield .**
Right: **River Allen from Cupola Bridge.**

Downstream, past the Cupola Bridge, the Allen enters the spectacular Starward Gorge and perched high above, on a rocky promontory, stand the dramatic ruins of a medieval tower known as Starward Pele. Tumbling on past the delightful picnic areas of Plankey Mill and Allenbanks, the river Allen finally joins the South Tyne between Bardon Mill and Haydon Bridge.

Above: **John Dodd, one of 'The Last Horsemen'**

WEARDALE

At Wearhead, the mighty river Wear begins life as a gurgling, moorland trickle. Winding its way past the lonely hill farms that are scattered across the rugged moorland of the North Pennines, the trickle is fed by numerous sparkling burns and linns and quickly begins to grow.

Gathering momentum, the river tumbles ever eastwards down the Wear valley, passing through an unfolding panorama of lush pasturelands, picturesque hamlets, historic chapels and bustling market towns. Rich in culture and tradition, this is Weardale, the Land of the Prince Bishops.

One of Weardale's most impressive industrial legacies and certainly one of the most visited, is the Killhope Wheel, at the North of England Lead Mining Museum. 40ft in diameter and built to power ore crushing machinery, the water driven wheel, which is the centrepiece of the museum, has been fully restored to its original working splendour. The wheel was powered by water held in a dam on the fells above, and was led to the wheel through a system of wooden troughs, supported on stone plinths.

Now, after years of careful restoration, visitors to Killhope can experience an atmospheric reconstruction of daily life in a 19th century leadmine. Well informed guided tours of the

Above: **The River Wear meanders through Pennine farmland near Wearhead.**

site are available, both underground and on the surface and include demonstrations of the ingenious, water powered processes that were used to drive the machinery and wash, grade and separate the lead ore from the impurities.

The museum also houses a fascinating collection of "spar

North of England Lead Mining Museum, Killhope.

boxes". Beautifully crafted by leadminers in days gone by and now prized family heirlooms, these unique showcases were used to display the sparkling crystals that miners occasionally came across whilst working underground.

Many visitors continue their journey down Weardale with a visit to the Weardale museum at Ireshopeburn. This small folk museum offers visitors a vivid insight into the religious and domestic aspects of life in the dale around the turn of the century. Next to the museum is High House Methodist Chapel. Founded in 1760, John Wesley preached here and this is now the world's oldest Methodist chapel still in continuous weekly use.

Further downriver stands the village of St. Johns Chapel, scene of the annual Weardale Agricultural Show. The present church stands on the site of a Chapel of Ease used in the early 13th century by Durham's Prince Bishops.

Having been invested with the trappings of kingship by William the Conqueror in 1080, Durham's Prince Bishops

were allowed to behave in a truly regal manner and in return for this unique arrangement, they acted as England's buffer against the ever present threat of Scottish invasion. Their power base was the castle at Durham, and the magnificent Cathedral served as their church.

In addition to Weardale, their vast estates, known as the Palatinate, stretched far into Northumberland and North Yorkshire. Holding court in their palace at Bishop Auckland, they appointed their own judges and administered both civil and criminal justice. They were also empowered to raise armies, create barons, charter markets and mint their own currency. The bishops even commissioned their own version of the Domesday Book. Known as the Boldon Book, it dates from the 12th century and mentions many of the area's historic villages and distinctive, open greens.

By the beginning of the 14th century, Durham's Prince Bishops were a major power within the realm and were regarded by many as the second kings of England. At times however, relations between the king and the Bishops inevitably became strained and on occasion, power was temporarily taken over by the crown. In later centuries, Durham's Prince Bishops became widely criticised for their flamboyant lifestyle and by the 17th century, much of their power had been for stripped away.

In 1987 however, the Bishops made something of a comeback when their unique image became the inspiration

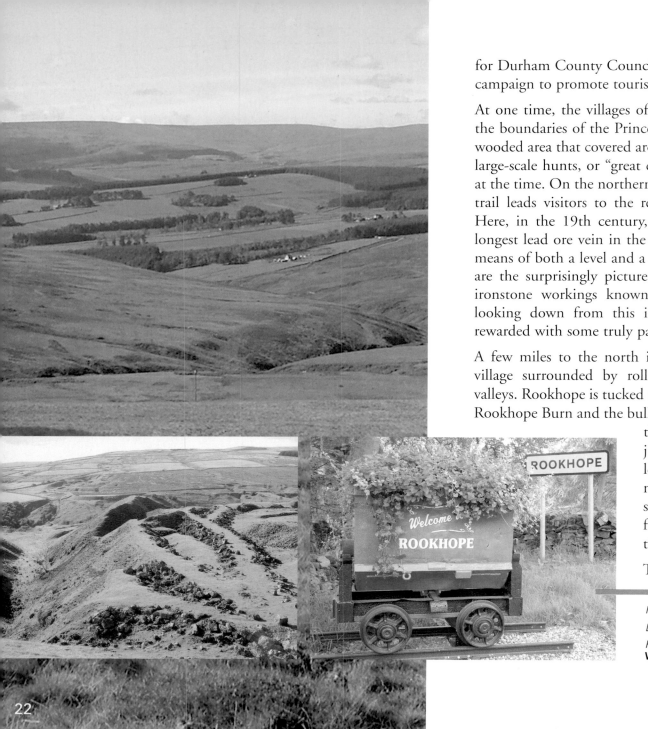

for Durham County Council's 'Land of the Prince Bishops' campaign to promote tourism in the area.

At one time, the villages of Westgate and Eastgate marked the boundaries of the Prince Bishop's deer park. Here, in a wooded area that covered around 13 miles, the Bishops held large-scale hunts, or "great chases", as they were referred to at the time. On the northern slopes above Westgate, a scenic trail leads visitors to the remains of the Low Slitt Mine. Here, in the 19th century, the Slitt Vein, which was the longest lead ore vein in the North Pennines, was mined by means of both a level and a shaft. Higher up on the hillside are the surprisingly picturesque remnants of the opencast ironstone workings known as West Rigg Opencut, and looking down from this intriguing site, visitors will be rewarded with some truly panoramic views of Weardale.

A few miles to the north is Rookhope, a charming dales village surrounded by rolling moors and lush, wooded valleys. Rookhope is tucked away in the upper reaches of the Rookhope Burn and the bulk of the village nestles snugly on the north banks of the river. At just over 1,000 feet above sea level, Rookhope's high altitude makes for a short growing season, resulting in a glorious floral display along the sides of the sparkling burn.

This captivating dales village

Main Photo: **Wear Valley**.

Left: **Welcome to Rookhope**.

Far left: **Remnants of Ironstone workings at West Rigg Opencut**.

Above: **Remaining arch from the Lintzgarth Smelt Mill.**

also has the distinction of being the earliest site of metal mining in the Pennines. In 1153, King Stephen granted permission to mine iron and lead here and by the beginning of the 14th century, "farmer-miners" were searching for lead deposits in riverbeds and streams. For centuries, this combination of mining and farming sustained a thriving population and the area is dotted with pits and leadmines, some with intriguing names such as Bowk's Level, Seeing Sike and Harry's Hush. 'Hushing' was a process which involved damming a promising stream, or 'sike' and when a large enough head of water had collected, it was then suddenly released. The resulting downpour washed away the surface soil, and hopefully, exposed veins of lead bearing ore.

On the road to Allenheads can be seen the only remaining arch, one of six, which carried a horizontal stone flue from Lintzgarth Smelt Mill out onto the open moors. This flue was an enormous length, and in addition to drawing off and discharging poisonous fumes from the lead furnaces at what was deemed a safe distance, it also provided the necessary draught to keep the smelters blazing. The flue also caught precious deposits of lead and silver that had been sucked out of the smelt mill, and at weekends, boys were sent in to sweep it out. We can only wonder what those poor lads were paid for doing such a filthy, dangerous job.

Rookhope has also been immortalised in one of the most famous of the "Border Ballads" - The Rookhope Ryde. Although the Durham dales may seem a long way from the war-torn Anglo Scottish borderland of the 16th century, it would appear they were far from immune to the depredations of the notorious Border Reivers. In the year 1569, we are told, raiders from the Bewcastle Wastes crossed over Rookhope Head and proceeded to "reive" 600 sheep. However, as they quietly departed with their woolly plunder,

they were unlucky enough to be spotted, and amidst hue and cry, were pursued by a posse of Rookhope men led by George Emmerson, the Bailiff of Eastgate. The Rookhope lads overtook the startled thieves and in the ensuing affray, the raiders suffered a number of fatal casualties, and had to limp back home emptyhanded.

Further down the valley stands the town of Stanhope, "Queen of the Dales".

A good place to start your visit to Stanhope is the Durham Dales Centre, which you can find in the former gardens of Stanhope Castle. Here, in this delightful setting, you will find the helpful and well-equipped Tourist Information Centre. The building is also home to some fine local craft galleries and a very tempting tearoom, where visitors can sample some splendid home cooking. Afterwards, you might just want to find a sunny corner in the charming Dales garden, and simply relax.

Lead and iron were smelted in Stanhope and the 'Stanhope and Tyne Railway', which opened in 1834, was the highest standard gauge railway in England and carried limestone across the moors to the steelworks of Consett, Tyneside and Cleveland. The town's prosperity in the 19th century is reflected in some of its rather grand Victorian buildings and although Stanhope no longer has a market, there is still a reminder in the shape of a fine stone cross.

On the north side of the market square stands

Main photo: **Evening light above Rookhope.**

Left: **Durham Dales Centre, Stanhope.**

St. Thomas's Church. At the base of its Norman tower lie a number of grave covers dating from the 13th century and alongside them is a fine example of a medieval stone coffin, constructed from Frosterley marble. Inside the church, the Victorian font is also carved from Frosterley marble, as is the altar dais and border. In the churchyard is Stanhope's remarkable Fossilised Tree. Two hundred and fifty million years ago, in the Carboniferous Period, this giant tree once grew and then died in a vast, primeval forest. As the vegetable matter decayed, it was replaced by minerals, which formed a perfect cast of the tree stump, in hard ganister.

Fronting the market place is Stanhope Castle. Built in 1798 on the site of an earlier ruined castle, it has seen many uses and has served as a county seat, a shooting lodge, an approved school and a museum.

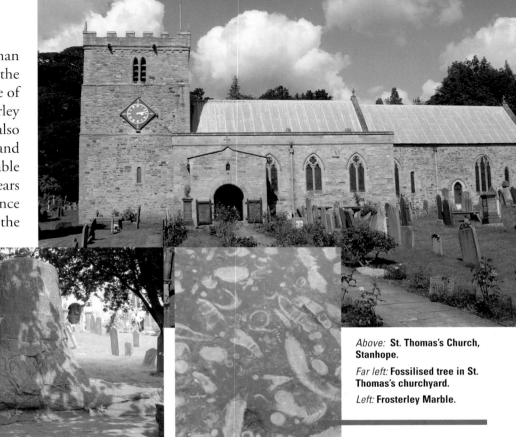

Above: **St. Thomas's Church, Stanhope.**

Far left: **Fossilised tree in St. Thomas's churchyard.**

Left: **Frosterley Marble.**

Above the Stanhope Burn is the strongly fortified manor house of Stanhope Hall. From the 12th century, it was home to the Featherstonehaughs, local gentry who held it until 1704, when the last of the line died fighting in Austria, alongside the Duke of Marlborough.

Nearby is the town's elegant rectory. Originally built in 1697, it was rebuilt in 1821 at a cost of £12,000, a princely sum in those days, which reflected the considerable wealth of the established church. In Weardale, much of that wealth came from the toil of local leadminers, who were obliged to pay heavy tithes to the rector, and at the beginning of the 19th century, Stanhope was probably the richest rectorship in England. Disillusioned by the greed of the church, the leadminers detested this iniquitous arrangement and in the 1740's, crowds of them flocked to hear Wesley's sermons and the creed of Methodism spread rapidly through the dales.

In 1847, a railway line built by the Stockton and Darlington Railway Company followed the path of the River Wear and linked the villages of Wearhead, Stanhope, Frosterley and

Wolsingham with Bishop Auckland. Originally built to transport limestone to the ironworks on Teesside, the line survived into more modern times as a passenger service, but this was withdrawn in 1953 and the line was finally closed down in 1993.

In 2004, however, after much hard work by the Weardale Railway Trust, part of the line was re-opened. Stations at Stanhope, Frosterley and Wolsingham have been refurbished and a variety of restored steam trains now provide a heritage railway service. Passengers can once again enjoy fine views of Weardale on the five-mile ride from Stanhope, calling at Frosterley and Wolsingham.

To the west of the town, a path winds through the delightful woods of Stanhope Dene. Here, in 1843 at Heathery Burn, workmen building a tramway for a nearby limestone quarry broke through a cave and unearthed a fabulous horde of Bronze Age weapons, ornaments and tools. These priceless artifacts are now on show at the British Museum, but unfortunately, over the years, the cave itself eventually fell victim to further quarrying.

Further down the dale is the delightful village of Frosterley. Probably of Saxon origin, the village is first mentioned in the Boldon Book, in 1183. The name was formerly 'forest lea', a reference to the fact that this area was once prime deer

Top: **Frosterley.**
Above: **Mardy Monster, Wolsingham Station.**

hunting country. Nowadays, little of that forest remains and since the 13th century, the land surrounding Frosterley has been extensively quarried. Huge limestone quarries can be seen to the south of the village, and there are also a number of large, disused limekilns nearby, such as the stone built range at White Kirkley. This area is also famous for its so-called 'marble'. Exported worldwide, 'Frosterley Marble' is in fact a decorative black limestone, and since medieval times, has been used extensively throughout the county. It can be seen to advantage in Durham Cathedral and in the Chapel at Auckland Castle.

To the east of Frosterley stands the town of Wolsingham. Once a thriving market town established by the Prince Bishops, it is still home to Englands oldest agricultural show, always held on the first Saturday in September. Behind the church of St. Mary and St. Stephen lies a former rectory, which was used by the Prince Bishops to house guests attending their hunts.

The ironworks at the eastern end of the town were built by Charles Attwood, a former glass maker and entrepreneur from Worcestershire. Having leased the right to mine ironstone in the manors of Stanhope and Wolsingham, Attwood went into partnership with the Baring brothers and established the Weardale Iron Company at nearby Tow Law. After his retirement, Attwood successfully patented his own steelmaking process and opened the iron works at Stanners Close, turning iron into steel.

To the north of Wolsingham, in the Tunstall Valley near Waskerley Beck, is the ancient oak wood at Backstone Bank. This was originally part of Wolsingham Park and from 1247, was maintained by the Bishop of Durham's Master Foresters and Parkers. Over the centuries, the history of this forest was well documented and we know that the area was successfully planted and replanted, making this one of the few forests in the county that allows us a glimpse of medieval woodland management.

Perched high above the valley stand the ruins of a pele tower at Baal Hill. Home to the bailiff of Wolsingham Park, the tower was robustly constructed in much the same way as its cousins on the Scottish border and was built to repel raiders and thieves - both Scots and English.

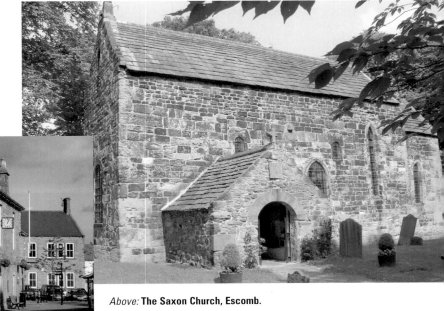

Above: **The Saxon Church, Escomb.**
Left: **Wolsingham.**

At the head of the valley is the Tunstall Reservoir. Built in 1879 to supply industry in the towns of Spennymoor, Willington and Shildon, it later served the mining communities of southwest Durham. Nowadays, it is a popular venue for anglers.

To the south is Hamsterley Forest, where visitors can follow quiet footpaths through wooded glades, and simply enjoy the peace and sheer tranquillity of this rich and diverse woodland.

over the centuries, but they do not detract from the peace and serenity that visitors will always find in the church's venerable interior.

As the Wear winds southeast, it passes near the beautiful Saxon church at Escomb. Although no one is quite sure when the church was built, its similarity to the churches at Monkwearmouth and Jarrow would suggest the 7th century. There are no great saints associated with the church and we do not know who built it. Ironically, it is perhaps this obscurity that has led to its survival as the most complete Anglo Saxon church in England. Sympathetically restored, Escomb is one of the finest examples of early Christian architecture in Northern Europe. With the exception of the upper walls, all the stones used to build the church were taken from the former Roman fort at nearby Binchester. Above the porch a serpent decorates one of the country's finest surviving Saxon sundials. Indoors, on the underside of the chancel arch, there are the remains of a 12th century painting and behind the altar table, there is a fragment of a Saxon carved stone cross.

There have been some minor features added to the church

Downriver, to the north of Bishop Auckland, stand the remains of the Roman fort of Binchester. Once the largest Roman fort in County Durham, it was built in the 2nd century AD and guarded the point where Dere Street crossed the River Wear. The fort was defended by a wall 5 metres high and its gateways were flanked by guard towers and a steep, V-shaped ditch.

The house of the forts' commander also boasts the finest example in Britain of a Roman military bath suite. The Romans eventually abandoned the fort around 410AD and in time, the buildings were systematically plundered for their dressed stonework.

As the river continues its journey eastwards, curling proudly around Durham's towering Cathedral and flowing on to the North Sea, we take our leave of Weardale, Land of the Prince Bishops - its traditions, landscape and history second to none.

TEESDALE

High in the Northern Pennines, the river Tees rises on Cross Fell, an area of sweeping, heather, clad moorland. In the summer months it is a mecca for hillwalkers, but in winter, this landscape can become wild, bleak and unforgiving.

Cutting its way through the rugged moorland, the young Tees tumbles past scattered, white painted cottages, and into the broad expanse of Cow Green Reservoir. The largest of 6 reservoirs in Teesdale, it took 3 years to complete and serves the thriving conurbations of Darlington and Teeside. Here, on the surrounding moors, botanists trek the fells in search of blue gentian and other rare alpines that survive from the ice age.

Below Cow Green, the Tees cascades down through Cauldron Snout, a narrow gap in the black, dolerite rock. Nearby, nestling under the dark bulk of Cronkley Scar, is the little hamlet of Langdon Beck, a welcome haven for walkers bound for upper Teesdale.

Main photo: **Cow Green Reservoir, Upper Teesdale.**
Inset photos: Left to right: **High Cup Nick, Cauldron Snout, High Force, Low Force.**

Wynch Bridge.

Newbiggin Chapel notice board.

Newbiggin Chapel.

Gathering pace, the river surges on to spectacularly plunge 70 ft over a black, Whin Sill cliff. This is High Force, England's highest waterfall, a truly awesome sight and one of the area's main attractions. Further down the valley, the river gushes through picturesque Low Force, a popular picnicking spot for locals and visitors alike.

Further downriver is the Bowlees Visitor Centre, from which a nearby path leads to the Wynch Bridge. The original bridge, built by leadminers, was thought to be the first suspension bridge in Europe, but in 1802, it collapsed and was replaced with the present structure.

Evidence of John Wesley and the dales Methodist legacy also abounds. At nearby Newbiggin stands a Methodist chapel built in 1759 and said to be the oldest surviving chapel in the country still being used to hold services.

The Tees flows on through a landscape patterned with dry stone walls and fields strewn with wild flowers, before reaching the town of Middleton-in-Teesdale. Called the 'Capital of Upper Teesdale' the town is a perfect centre for exploring the dales and was once an important centre for the leadmining industry. The Quaker London Leadmining Company thrived here in the early 19th century and in return for an austere life of sobriety and backbreaking work, built its workers cottages, a school and an ornate drinking fountain. Also worth visiting is the pretty 12th century church of St. Mary's.

Further downriver is the idyllic village of Romaldkirk which boasts not one, but three village greens, a fine waterpump

Above: **Romaldkirk.**   *Right:* **Quaker drinking fountain, Middleton-in-Teesdale.**

and a set of stocks. There is much to admire in this classic dales village and visitors can visit the beautiful 12th century church of St. Romald, known locally as the 'Cathedral of the Dales'. The village also has two fine public houses, both renowned for their hospitality, traditional ales and fine cuisine.

A short distance downstream from Romaldkirk stands the delightful village of Cotherstone, where dry stone walls and fragrant hay meadows nudge shoulders with lovingly tended cottage gardens. As in Romaldkirk, many of the houses are traditionally built from sun mellowed, local stone, some dating as far back as the 16th and 17th century. John Wesley preached in Cotherstone and the Methodist chapel was built in 1782. There are beautiful walks along the riverside and

just a short walk from the village is the picturesque site of a 13th century castle at Hagg Bank.

Cotherstone is also home to a famous daughter of the dales, Hannah Hauxwell, who became well known through a series of television documentaries that told the story of her life at Low Birk Hatt farm in Baldersdale.

For many years, on an income of less than £300 a year, Hannah lived in an isolated farmhouse without the benefit of electricity or running water. Her life was one of unremitting hardship, scraping together a meagre existence by renting out her fields for grazing and by occasionally parting with one of her beloved cows.

The stoic way in which this remarkably wise and serene lady accepted the challenges and rigours of such a harsh way of

Left: **The River Tees near Forest-in-Teesdale.**
Above left: **Cotherstone.**
Above right: **Hannah Hauxwell.**

life warmed the hearts of the nation and made her a national treasure.

As the years advanced, Hannah finally became unable to manage her farm and eventually chose to settle in Cotherstone. Still a countrywoman at heart, she rarely misses her daily walk along the winding footpaths that pass by the green meadows and stone barns which skirt this charming village.

The Tees flows swiftly onwards, reaching the fine market town of Barnard Castle 'The Gateway to Teesdale'. The town has been recognised nationally as one of the fifty-one most historically and architecturally important towns in Great Britain.

Above left: **Fly agaric.**
Above: **Stone barn.**
Right: **Teesdale meadow.**

Above: **Barnard Castle**.

Still guarded by the impressive remains of it's 12th century castle, 'Barney' as the town is affectionately known, has a wide variety of shops and facilities and each Wednesday, hosts a lively farmers market. Tree lined Galgate features some attractive buildings and follows the line of a Roman road, which crossed the Tees by a ford 120 metres upstream from the castle.

The "Butter Market", or Market Cross, has been a focal point in the town for over 250 years. Built by Thomas Breaks and given to the town in 1747, it has been used as a Town Hall, a Court Leet and a 'lock up'. The weather vane has two bullet holes through it, being the legacy of a shooting contest in 1804 between a soldier and a

gamekeeper. The Bank was once the town's main commercial street and some Victorian window fronts still survive.

The oldest inhabited building in 'Barney' is Blagraves House. Built in the 16th century, Oliver Cromwell was entertained here and the building has seen service as a ropeworks, an inn and a museum.

Standing high above the Tees, the castle, built by Bernard Baliol in the 12th century (hence "Bernard's" Castle) was later seized by one of Durham's Prince Bishops and in 1569, played a significant part in the defeat of the northern earls who rose against Elizabeth I. The ruins incorporate an impressive curtain wall and a fine round tower.

Beneath the castle and spanning the Tees is County Bridge, which reached its present form in 1569. Once the meeting point of two counties and the lands of two bishops, it was a venue for illicit weddings, which were held in the bridge's centre, where neither bishop would object. Public footpaths follow the riverbank and offer superb views of the dale, castle and town.

In the 18th and 19th century, nearby Thorngate and Bridgegate were the sites of the town's industrial area. In Thorngate, weavers houses have been converted into fashionable dwellings and now, grassy slopes cover the remains of the riverside woollen mills and the small, cramped houses that accommodated their workers.

St. Mary's church, built in the 12th century, has a fine Norman doorway and incorporates many architectural features from later periods.

A quarter of a mile east of the town centre stands the imposing Bowes Museum. Built on the lines of a French chateau, it houses a display of beautiful furniture, paintings and ceramics from the second Napoleonic Empire period. Most of the items in the museum were collected by John Bowes and his French wife Josephine. Sadly, neither of them lived to witness

Above: **Market Cross, Barnard Castle**
Left: **The oldest inhabited building in Barnard Castle, Blagraves House.**

Above and left: **Bowes Museum**.

the opening of their museum in 1892. Perhaps the most popular object in the museum is the mechanical silver swan which, when activated appears to dip it's head, take a fish from the water and swallow it.

A few miles south west of Barnard Castle lies the historic village of Bowes. It's castle, which stands on the site of a Roman fort, was built for Henry II between 1171 and 1187 and guarded the approach to Stainmore Pass. The massive 12th century stone keep, which overlooks the valley of the

Above: **The 12th century keep, Bowes Castle.**

Right: **Ruins of Egglestone Abbey.**

river Greta, is partly constructed of re-used stones from the Roman fort.

To the south east of 'Barney', across a quaint medieval pack horse bridge, are the picturesque ruins of Egglestone Abbey. Founded in 1190 by the Premonstratensians, the Abbey suffered frequent damage from both Scots and English armies and after the Dissolution, in 1538, some of the buildings were converted into a manorial hall.

Nearby stands the impressive 18th century mansion house known as Rokeby Hall. When Sir Walter Scott was a guest here, the building and surrounding landscape inspired him to write the poem, 'Rokeby'. Behind the hall runs the river Greta and before flowing into the Tees, it passes under Dairy Bridge, a delicate structure much favoured by local artists.

Near the banks of the Tees stands the tiny Wycliffe Church, where John Wycliffe, who went on to translate the Bible into English, is reputed to have been born.

Northeast of Barnard Castle stands the charming village of Staindrop which has a fine church with a Norman tower and monuments to the Neville family, once proud rulers of nearby Raby Castle.

The Nevilles lost possession of Raby Castle due to their part in 'the Rising of the North' in 1569 and since 1626, the fortress has remained in the hands of Lord Barnard's family. Surrounded by spacious parklands, this magnificent 14th century fortress boasts 9 towers, a medieval kitchen, an octagonal drawing room and a collection of sumptuous period furniture and rare paintings. The stables house a fine collection of horse drawn carriages and large herds of red and fallow deer roam the expansive parklands. Visitors can also relax in the delightfully laid-out walled garden.

To the north of Raby Castle is the Gaunless Valley.

Below: **Raby Castle**.

Above: **The village green, Staindrop.**

Above: **Chimney at the site of Copely Smelt Mill.**

'Gaunless' is a celtic word meaning worthless and apparently, in early times, the area was forsaken. However, by the medieval period, men were exploiting the rich seams of coal and iron ore that lay just beneath the thin clay soil and soon the landscape was peppered with drift mines and bell pits.

By the 19th century there was a profusion of collieries, coke ovens, brick kilns and lead smelting mills, all serviced by a network of packhorse trails and railway lines. That once flourishing industry is now a thing of the past, but visitors can still explore the legacy of this vibrant period. The remains of old coke ovens still survive near Butterknowle and the site of the Smelt Mill at Copley is well worth a visit.

The village of Cockfield was home to the renowned surveyor, Jeremiah Dixon, a famous son of Teesdale. In

Above: **Cockfield Fell.**

1763, Dixon sailed to North America with his companion Charles Mason and by surveying the famous Mason-Dixon line, settled a boundary dispute between the states of Pennsylvania and Maryland.

Nearby, lies Cockfield Fell, an archaeological site of national importance and one of the earliest industrial landscapes in Britain. Once the workplace of quarrymen, engineers, miners and farmers, this breezy, open hillside is now littered with grass-covered humps and hollows. These are the remnants of dozens of small quarries and bell pits, which lie alongside traces of earlier Bronze Age and Iron Age field systems.

As the Tees flows eastwards, it passes the historic village of Gainford, where tasteful Georgian houses cluster round the village green. Nearby, is Gainford Hall, an impressive 16th century manor house that has a picturesque stone dovecote in its grounds. The village is also known for being the place where the comedian Stan Laurel received his education, at the Gainford Academy.

As the river approaches Darlington, our journey down the Tees brings us to Piercebridge. This charming village stands on the site of a Roman fort built to guard Dere Street, the Roman road to the north. Nowadays, traditional cottages overlook the pleasant village green and a graceful bridge spans the sparkling river Tees.

Above: **Gainford Village green.**
Right: **16th Century manor house, Gainford Hall.**

And so, we take our leave of the North Pennines. Here, in these lush, green valleys and lofty, rolling moorlands, you'll find a rare combination of unspoilt beauty, romantic history and a quite unique industrial heritage. There's so much to explore and enjoy. It's no wonder that visitors keep coming back - again and again.